Pupil Book 6
Composition

Author: Chris Whitney

Published by Collins
An imprint of HarperCollinsPublishers
The News Building
1 London Bridge Street
London
SE1 9GF

Browse the complete Collins catalogue at
www.collins.co.uk

© HarperCollinsPublishers Limited 2015

10 9 8 7 6 5 4 3

ISBN 978-0-00-813349-8

British Library Cataloguing in Publication Data
A Catalogue record for this publication is available from the British Library

Publishing Manager: Tom Guy
Project Managers: Dawn Booth and Kate Ellis
Editor: Hannah Hirst-Dunton
Cover design and artwork: Amparo Barrera
Internal design concept: Amparo Barrera
Typesetting: Jouve India Private Ltd
Illustrations: Dante Ginevra, Aptara and QBS

Printed in Italy by Grafica Veneta S.p.A.

Acknowledgements

Macmillan Publishers Ltd for the poem "The Wind and the Sun" by Julia Donaldson, from *Crazy Mayonnaisy Mum* written by Julia Donaldson, copyright © Macmillan Children's Books, 2005; Egmont UK Ltd for an extract from *Flat Stanley* by Jeff Brown, text copyright © 1964 The Trust u/w/o Richard Brown a/k/a Jeff Brown f/b/o Duncan Brown. Illustration copyright © 2006 Scott Nash. Published by Egmont UK Ltd and used with permission; and Julie Holder for the poem "The Loner" by Julie Holder, published in *Poetry Book, 3rd edition*, edited by John Foster, Oxford University Press, 1982. Reproduced by kind permission of Julie Holder

(t = top, b = bottom)

p. 28 NASA; p. 48 (t) Clive Brunskill/Getty Images; p. 48 (b) Clive Brunskill/Getty Images; p. 50 (t) Ezra Shaw/Getty Images; p. 50 (b) Ezra Shaw/Getty Images; p. 57 (t) Lee Frost/Getty Images; p. 57 (b) Visions of our Land/Getty Images; p. 60 (t) Peter Adams/Getty Images; p. 60 (b) Per-Andre Hoffman/Getty Images

MIX
Paper from
responsible sources
FSC C007454

Contents

Story planning

When planning a story, you should decide on settings, characters and plot. You should also try to have a clear idea of why you are writing. It might be just to entertain, but there are other things stories can achieve as well. Here's a plan Charles Dickens could have made for his story 'Oliver Twist'.

Read the text below, then answer the questions that follow.

Stories can have many settings.

Settings

- a workhouse
- an orphanage
- an undertaker's shop
- London – Fagin's house
- London – Mr Brownlow's house

Characters

- Oliver Twist: a young orphan – the hero of the story
- Mr Bumble (parish beadle): a cruel man, treats Oliver badly
- Mr Sowerberry (undertaker): also cruel to Oliver, who is apprenticed to him
- Jack Dawkins (Artful Dodger): befriends Oliver, takes him to Fagin
- Fagin: a criminal who trains orphaned boys to steal for him
- Mr Brownlow: a kindly gentleman (revealed to be Oliver's grandfather)
- Bill Sikes: a violent criminal associate of Fagin's
- Mrs Maylie: a kindly lady whose house Sikes burgles

Plot

- Oliver born in workhouse – mother dies – grows up in orphanage
- Apprenticed to cruel undertaker – runs away to London

- Meets Artful Dodger who takes him to Fagin – sent to learn to steal
- Oliver framed for theft in street, caught by police – Mr Brownlow saves him, takes him home
- Oliver abducted by Bill Sikes – forced to burgle house – shot in act but rescued by Mrs Maylie, taken to countryside
- Sikes, fleeing angry mob, has fatal accident, Fagin caught and hanged for crimes
- Oliver reunited with grandfather, Mr Brownlow

Audience

- Readers of 'Bentley's Miscellany'

Purpose

- To entertain and excite the readers (and thereby sell more papers)
- To show the readers the terrible state of the poor
- To inspire the readers to make changes to help the poor

Strategy (how to achieve my purpose)

To entertain and excite (and sell more papers) I will:

- Create characters the readers will love
- Write scenes of drama and action
- Include action, tragedy and humour
- Introduce plenty of mystery, intrigue and suspense
- End chapters on cliff-hangers

To describe poverty and inspire change I will:

- Use wit and humour to expose injustice
- Create a poor main character that readers will feel sorry for and want to help
- Set my story here and now – it's about the problems we have today
- Use realism so the readers know, even though it's a story, these things can and do happen.

Get started

Discuss these questions and complete the tasks with a partner.

Can you think of any books that you've read where the chapters end right in the middle of an exciting part? Can you think of any television programmes that finish their episodes like this? Discuss these chapter and episode endings. What was happening? Why was it so exciting? What is this type of ending called? What effect does it have on the reader or viewer?

Try these

Answer these questions about the story plan for 'Oliver Twist'.

1. Name two adult characters in 'Oliver Twist' who are on the side of good.

2. Name four cruel characters in 'Oliver Twist'.

3. What are the different settings in 'Oliver Twist'?

4. What should you consider when writing a story?

5. Who were the intended readers of 'Oliver Twist'?

6. How has this story plan been organised?

7. What were the reasons Dickens wrote 'Oliver Twist'?

8. Why does Dickens often leave Oliver in difficult situations at the ends of chapters?

9. What bad thing happens to Oliver after these good things happened to him?

   • Oliver runs away to London and meets the Artful Dodger but ...

   • Oliver is saved from the police by Mr Brownlow but ...

Now try these

1. What issues or injustices would you like to expose? Could you write a story to inspire your readers to solve or change things? Plan an inspiring story about something happening in the world today that you would like to see solved or changed. Copy and complete the story-planning table to help you. You can choose one of these topics, or use an idea of your own.

   • Saving the rainforest

   • Global warming

   • Child labour

Topic: (What will you tell your readers about?)
Settings: (Where is the problem you are writing about?)
Characters: (Include some nice and some nasty characters. Who is the main character? Who will the readers identify with? Will there be any misunderstood characters?)
Plot: (How will the storyline persuade or inspire your readers?)
Strategy: (How will you make your readers care about your topic?)

2. Authors often spend a long time researching the topic they are writing about to help them get the details of the story right and to help them decide exactly what it is they want to say. Spend time researching your topic and find out as much as you can about it. Go back to your story plan and check that all your ideas still work with what you know now. Make any changes you need to and add any ideas you have had as a result of your research. When you are ready, write a scene from your story. It can be the beginning, or any other scene that is particularly clear in your mind.

Summaries

A summary is a shortened version of a piece of writing which includes the most important details. Here's an extract from **'Peter Pan' by J.M. Barrie**. (Nana is a dog employed as the children's nanny.)

Read the extract from **'Peter Pan' by J.M. Barrie**, and the summary of the extract, then answer the questions that follow.

On the night we speak of, all the children were once more in bed. It happened to be Nana's evening off, and Mrs Darling had bathed them and sung to them until one by one they had let go of her hand and slid away into the land of sleep.

All were looking so safe and cosy that she sat down tranquilly by the fire to sew. The fire was warm, however, and the nursery dimly lit by three night-lights, and presently the sewing lay on Mrs Darling's lap. Then her head nodded. She was asleep.

While she slept she had a dream. She dreamt that the Neverland had come too near, and that a strange boy had broken through from it.

The dream by itself would have been a trifle, but while she was dreaming the window from the nursery blew open, and a boy did drop on the floor. He was accompanied by a strange light, no bigger than your fist, which darted about the room like a living thing; and I think it must have been this light that must have wakened Mrs Darling.

She started up with a cry, and saw the boy, and somehow she knew at once that he was Peter Pan.

Mrs Darling screamed, and, as if in answer to a bell, the door opened, and Nana entered, returning from her evening out. She growled and sprang at the boy, who leapt lightly through the window. Again, Mrs Darling screamed, this time in distress for him for she thought he was killed, and she ran down into the street to look for his little body, but it was not there; and she looked up, and in the black night she could see nothing but what she thought was a shooting star.

She returned to the nursery, and found Nana with something in her mouth, which proved to be the boy's shadow. As he had leapt at the window Nana had closed it quickly, too late to catch him but his shadow had not had time to get out; slam went the window and snapped it off.

She decided to roll it up and put it away carefully in a drawer, until a fitting opportunity came for telling her husband.

Summary

Don't include unnecessary descriptive details.

If you use exact text from the story, put it in quotation marks.

English is simplest in the present tense so it's useful for writing summaries.

Never copy out whole sentences.

Paraphrase (use your own words) for the most efficient language.

The story of 'Peter Pan' opens when the children are asleep. Nana is out, and Mrs Darling has fallen asleep over her sewing. While she is dreaming about a "strange boy" from "Neverland", he arrives in the nursery accompanied by a bright light. Mrs Darling wakes up and immediately knows it is Peter Pan. She screams just as Nana enters . Nana springs at the boy who leaps through the window. Mrs Darling goes outside to see if he is hurt but finds nothing. On returning to the nursery, she finds Nana has trapped Peter's shadow, so she puts it in a drawer.

Dialogue can be written as reported speech to save space.

Get started

Discuss these questions and complete the tasks with a partner.

1. Think of a film you have seen and describe it to your partner. Listen to your partner's description of a film. Discuss your descriptions. What details were included? What details were left out? What details were included that you could have left out? What were the most important details?

2. What is a summary? What should you try to achieve when writing a summary?

3. Write a summary of the film you described earlier. Pay close attention to what you include and what you leave out.

Try these

Answer these questions about writing summaries.

1. What are the five main points to remember when writing a summary? Make a list.

2. Rewrite these sentences in as few words as possible.

   a) All were looking so safe and cosy that she sat down tranquilly by the fire to sew.

   b) Mrs Darling screamed, and, as if in answer to a bell, the door opened, and Nana entered, returning from her evening out.

   c) As he had leapt at the window Nana had closed it quickly, too late to catch him but his shadow had not had time to get out; slam went the window and snapped it off.

3. What is direct speech? What is reported speech? Which is generally more useful in a summary?

4. Write a sentence to summarise each paragraph of the original text.

5. Summarise the summary by writing it as a list of events. Can you cut it down even more?

Now try these

1. Read this next extract from 'Peter Pan'. Then write a summary of it in no more than 50 words.

For a moment after Mr and Mrs Darling left the house the night-lights by the beds of the three children continued to burn clearly ... There was another light in the room now, a thousand times brighter than the night-lights, and in the time it has taken to say this, it has been in all the drawers in the nursery, looking for Peter's shadow, rummaging the wardrobe and turned every pocket inside out. It was not really a light; it made this light by flashing about so quickly; but when it came to rest for a second you saw it was a fairy, no bigger than your hand, but still growing. It was a girl called Tinker Bell.

A moment after the fairy's entrance the window was blown open by the breathing of the little stars and Peter flew in. "Tinker Bell," he called softly, after making sure that the children were asleep, "Tink, where are you?"

She was in a jug for the moment and liking it extremely; she had never been in a jug before.

"Oh, do come out of that jug, and tell me, do you know where they put my shadow?"

2. A blurb is a short description of a book, written to help people decide whether or not they want to read the book the blurb is about. Most blurbs summarise key information about the book, such as settings, characters, themes and a little bit of the plot. But the main aim of a blurb is always to persuade the reader that they really do want to read the book, so it can't give too much away. Choose a book that you have enjoyed and write a blurb for it. Summarise the key information and try to make the book sound really appealing. What information can you summarise about the book without giving too much away?

Adapting stories for plays

Well-known stories are often turned into playscripts for the stage or television. This extract is taken from **'Jane Eyre' by Charlotte Brontë**, published in 1847. Jane is an orphan. Her Aunt Reed, who has been looking after her, has invited Mr Brocklehurst of Lowood School to interview Jane to see if she is suitable for the school.

Read the extract from **'Jane Eyre' by Charlotte Brontë,** and the playscript adapted from it, then answer the questions that follow.

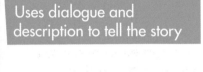
Uses dialogue and description to tell the story

Mrs Reed occupied her usual seat by the fireside; she made a signal for me to approach; I did so, and she introduced me to the stony stranger with the words –

"This is the girl respecting whom I applied to you."

He – for it was a man – turned his head slowly towards where I stood, and having examined me with two inquisitive looking grey eyes which twinkled under a pair of bushy eyebrows, said solemnly, and in a bass voice –

"Her size is small; what is her age?"

"Ten years."

"So much?" was the doubtful answer ...

"Your name, little girl?"

"Jane Eyre, sir" ...

"Well, Jane Eyre, are you a good child?" ...

First person; the narrator is a character

Mrs Reed answered for me by an expressive shake of the head, adding soon,

"Perhaps the less said on that subject the better, Mr Brocklehurst."

"Sorry to hear it! She and I must have some talk ... Come here."

Past tense; the narrator describes her childhood

Information in the novel that is absent from the playscript

I stepped across the rug; he placed me square and straight before him. What a face he had, now that it was almost level with mine! What a great nose! And what a mouth! And what large prominent teeth!

"No sight so sad as that of a naughty child," he began, "especially a naughty little girl. Do you know where the wicked go after death?"

"They go to hell," was my ready and orthodox answer.

"And what is hell? Can you tell me that?"

"A pit full of fire."

"And should you like to fall into that pit, and be burning there for ever?"

"No, sir."

This is how the extract from the book can be turned into a playscript. This is known as an adaptation; a text that has been changed to work in a new form or medium.

Scene: In the drawing room of Mrs Reed's house. She is seated by the fireside. Mr Brocklehurst is nearby. Jane has just entered and is by the door.

Stage directions are written in the present tense (because they are instructions).

Takes description from the novel to use as stage directions

Mrs Reed: (gesturing that Jane should approach) This is the girl respecting whom I applied to you.

Mr Brocklehurst: (turning his head to examine Jane) Her size is small; what is her age?

Mrs Reed: Ten years.

Mr Brocklehurst: (sounding doubtful) So much? Your name, little girl?

Jane: (sounding nervous) Jane Eyre, sir.

Mr Brocklehurst: (not unkindly) Well, Jane Eyre, are you a good girl?

Mrs Reed: (shaking her head) Perhaps the less said on that subject the better, Mr Brocklehurst.

Mr Brocklehurst: (more stern now) Sorry to hear it. She and I must have some talk. (He motions for Jane to come across to him.) Come here.

(Jane steps across the rug and Mr Brocklehurst places her directly in front of him. Jane is looking anxious.)

Dialogue taken directly from the novel

Mr Brocklehurst: No sight so sad as that of a naughty child, especially a naughty little girl. Do you know where the wicked go after death?

Jane: (nodding yes) They go to hell.

Mr Brocklehurst: And what is hell? Can you tell me that?

Jane: (confidently) A pit full of fire.

Some stage directions have been added by the writer of the play.

Mr Brocklehurst: (sounding menacing) And should you like to fall into that pit, and be burning there for ever?

Jane: (meekly) No, sir.

Get started

Discuss these questions and complete the tasks with a partner.

1. How easy is it to put these aspects of a novel into a playscript? Put them in order, with the easiest first.
   - What someone thinks
   - What someone does
   - What someone says

2. How have these parts of the novel been treated in the playscript?
   - "was the doubtful answer"
   - "was my ready and orthodox answer"

3. Which of these elements from the original text did not make it into the playscript in some form?
   - "usual seat"
   - "she made a signal for me to approach"
   - "Mrs Read answered for me by an expressive shake of the head"
   - "What a face he had, now that it was almost level with mine!"

4. What reasons might you have to leave out elements of the story you are adapting?

Try these

Complete these tasks.

1. Write these as lines of a playscript.

   - Fiona stared at him and said, 'Did you eat the biscuits?'

   - 'That is a problem,' Grandpa mused, scratching his chin. 'A dreadful problem.'

   - 'I won't say sorry, I won't!' screamed Penny, kicking the fence.

2. Match the feeling, as written in a novel, to the stage direction that could express it in a playscript.

   (Concentrating) (Trying not to laugh) (Shaking) (Sobbing)

   - She thought her heart would break.

   - I couldn't let him know that I thought it was funny.

   - John had never been so scared in his life.

   - Maria knew she had to get it right – it was so important.

3. Write a stage direction for each of these sentences.

   - Simret laughed as she read the note, threw it in the bin and set off for school.

   - Jake was bored. There was nothing on the television and he'd played all his games.

Now try these

1. Choose a book to adapt to a playscript and select a scene from the book. Make notes on any settings, characters and stage directions you will use.

2. Using your notes, write the playscript of your chosen scene. Remember to follow the rules for correctly writing and setting out a playscript:

   - Write the details of where the scene is set at the beginning.

   - Don't use speech marks to show who is speaking.

   - Write a name followed by a colon to show who speaks each line.

   - Start a new line each time a character starts to speak.

   - Write stage directions to tell the performers what to do.

Personification

Personification is a type of metaphor where non-human things are given human characteristics. Here are some examples of personification:

> the sun smiled
> the trees danced in the wind
> the flames climbed up the house

The sun didn't actually smile, or the trees dance, or the flames climb the house. Instead the writer is using figurative language to make these non-human things seem human. You can apply personification to an abstract idea such as hope or truth. Human qualities you can use include emotions, intentions and speech.

Read **'The Wind and the Sun' by Julia Donaldson**, then answer the questions that follow.

'The Wind and the Sun' by Julia Donaldson

Said the wind to the sun, "I can carry off kites
And howl down the chimney on blustery nights.
I can sail boats and set windmills in motion,
Rattle the windows and ruffle the oceans."

> And the old sun grinned
> At the wild winter wind.

Said the sun to the wind, "I turn night into day,
Ice into water and grass into hay.
I can melt puddles and open up roses.
I can paint rainbows and freckles on noses."

> And the old sun grinned
> At the wild winter wind.

Said the wind to the sun, "You'll be sorry you spoke.
Down on the road is a man with a cloak.
If you're so clever then let's see you prove it.
We'll take it in turns to see who can remove it."

And the old sun grinned
At the wild winter wind.

The wind blew the trees till the boughs bent
and broke.
He bowled the man's hat off and howled round
his cloak.
He blew and he blustered, he tossed and he
tugged it.
The man wrapped it round him and tightly he
hugged it.

And the old sun grinned
At the wild winter wind.

"Take a rest," said the sun. "Let me shine on
him now."
He shone till the man started mopping his brow.
The man settled down in the shade of some
boulders.
He undid his cloak and it slipped from his shoulders.

And the old sun grinned
At the wild winter wind.

You cannot apply personification to a person; they are already human.

Get started

Discuss these questions and complete the tasks with a partner.

1. Explain in your own words what is meant by 'personification'. Use a dictionary to check your definition.

2. Solve the riddle: I have hands on my face. I can't speak but I can tell you something. What am I?

3. Think of riddles for your partner to solve. Try to solve ones they think of for you. Take it in turns to solve each other's riddles.

Try these

Answer these questions and complete the tasks.

1. What two things are personified in the poem?

2. What human qualities can you use to create personification?

3. What human qualities are used to create personification in the poem?

4. Is it possible to use personification when describing humans?

5. How is the use of the word 'I' personification?

6. What abstract concept does each of these well-known characters personify? (Research them if you need to.) Copy and complete the table.

	The idea being personified	Description of the character
Father Time		
Mother Nature		
The Grim Reaper		
Lady Justice		
Uncle Sam		

Now try these

1. Explain why each phrase is an example of personification.

   - The stars danced playfully in the moonlit sky.

   - The words seemed to leap off of the page as she read the story.

   - The Christmas lights in the tree winked and sparkled.

2. Which verb provides the personification in each of the above examples?

3. Think of a verb for each of these inanimate objects to give them a human quality.

   - an avalanche

   - some car brakes

   - the moon

4. Write a sentence for each object or objects in question 3 showing the use of personification.

5. Write a descriptive paragraph, using as many examples of personification as you can, on one of these subjects:

   - a moonlit night

   - a storm at sea

   - a forest fire

Biography

A biography is an account of someone's life. There are many types of biography of various lengths. Diaries, memoirs, and autobiographies are all types of biography. (An autobiography is a biography written by the person it's about.) Here's a biography of the famous novelist, Charles Dickens.

Read the biography and the CV, then answer the questions that follow.

Date and place of birth

Parentage

Charles John Huffam Dickens was born on 7 February 1812 in Portsmouth. His father was John Dickens, a clerk in the Navy Office. His mother was called Elizabeth. During his childhood he moved to London, then to Chatham and back to London again.

Places of education

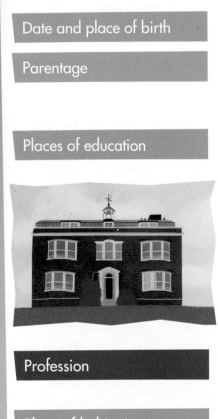

Dickens went to Rome Lane School and then Clover Lane School until 1821. At school he was very fond of reading. His education was cut short because his father was imprisoned for debt. Two days after his twelfth birthday, Dickens found himself working at Warren's blacking factory. When his father was released from prison, he sent Charles to Wellington House Academy to finish his education. He remained there until 1827.

Profession

Dickens then became a clerk for a firm of solicitors, learned shorthand and was promoted to court reporter. By 1832 he was writing for two journals and in 1833 he became a journalist for the newspaper the 'Morning Chronicle'. His job took him all over London and he enjoyed wandering about the city.

Place of habitation

Spouse's name and marriage date

In 1836 he married Catherine Hogarth and in the same year he became a well-known author when he wrote 'The Pickwick Papers'. From 1840 to 1841 he wrote two more of his famous novels, 'The Old Curiosity Shop' and 'Barnaby Rudge'.

In 1842 Dickens went to America. He travelled to New York, Philadelphia, Baltimore and Washington, as well as making a short trip to Canada, where he gave lectures to wide acclaim.

Hobbies and interests

One of his main interests in life was the theatre and he organised productions of plays at Knebworth House and Rockingham Castle.

In 1857 he moved to Gad's Hill in Kent and toured Switzerland, Italy and France.

In the 1860s he wrote some of his best work, 'Great Expectations', 'Our Mutual Friend' and the unfinished 'They Mystery of Edwin Drood'.

Major achievements

Date of death

He died in June 1870 and was buried at Westminster Abbey.

A curriculum vitae (CV for short) is a form of biographical writing that gives a brief account of a person's life, concentrating on education, qualifications and occupations. A CV is usually prepared for job applications.
Charles Dickens's CV may have looked something like this.

Date of birth

Place of habitation

Places of education

Professions

Surname: Dickens
Forenames: Charles John Huffam
Date of birth: 7.2.1812
Address: Gad's Hill, Kent
Education: 1881–1821 Rome Lane School
             1821–1824 Clover Lane School
             1825–1827 Wellington House Academy
Occupations: 1824 Warren's blacking factory
             1827 Clerk to a firm of solicitors
             Court reporter
             1832 Journalist – various journals
             1833 Journalist on the 'Morning Chronicle'
             1836 Novelist

Major achievements

Hobbies and interests

Hobbies: Walking
        Reading
        The theatre
        Travelling

Get started

Discuss these questions and complete the tasks with a partner.

1. Explain in your own words what is meant by the term 'biography'.

2. Give three examples of types of biographies that you may have read or learned about.

3. If you have read any biographies, whose life were they written about? If you haven't read a biography, do you know of any?

4. What is an autobiography? If you don't know, use a dictionary to find out.

5. Discuss any autobiographies that you have read or learned about.

Try these

Answer the questions and complete the tasks.

1. Where and when was Charles Dickens born?

2. What was the name and profession of Charles Dickens's father?

3. Why did Dickens have to work in Warren's blacking factory?

4. Who did Dickens marry and when did he marry her?

5. What countries did Dickens visit during his lifetime?

6. Write a timeline of Dickens's life.

7. What details would you expect to find in a biography? Make a list.

8. What is a curriculum vitae? What does it concentrate on?

9. Why would a curriculum vitae not include details of the person's death?

Now try these

1. Plan your own autobiography. Copy the table and complete it with important information about your life.

Date and place of birth:
Where I have been educated:
Places where I have lived:
Achievements so far:
Major events so far:
Any other important information:

2. Now write your autobiography. Remember to keep chronological order, to write in the first person and the past tense, and to organise your autobiography into paragraphs. Include lots of facts about your life and you can include your thoughts and feelings about your life too.

Factual writing

Much of the writing we do is based on facts (information that is known or proved to be true) and there are many different ways of presenting a factual piece of work.

Read the two different accounts of a science experiment, then answer the questions that follow.

Kate wrote a report on a science experiment and typed it out.

A statement of the aim

Aim

To find out how much foam is produced by mixing detergent with different types of water.

Equipment

glass jar containing liquid detergent:
pipette
test tube
bung
3 glass beakers with:
   river water
   sea water
   tap water

A set of instructions
(the order is very important)

Method

1 Half fill the test tube with river water.
2 Add 2 drops of detergent using the pipette.
3 Put the bung in the top of the test tube.
4 Shake for 10 seconds.
5 Leave to settle.
6 Record your results.
7 Repeat the method using sea water.
8 Repeat the method using tap water.

A table of results

Results

Water type	Amount of foam in cm
river water	6.5
sea water	4.5
tap water	10.5

Conclusion

The tap water produced the most foam and the sea water the least foam.

Lynn has written about the same science experiment in a different way.

Narrative of events

We had science today and Mr Simms was not in a good mood. We had to find out how much foam you got when you mixed detergent with different sorts of water. Mr Simms had got some river water, some sea water and some tap water. He said he had been to the seaside at the weekend to get the sea water.

Reported speech

Paragraphs

We had to get out lots of equipment. We needed test tubes and glass beakers and this thing you use to drop the detergent into water but I can't remember its name. We also had to have a bung to stick in the top of the test tube. I like saying the word "bung".

Irrelevant to the experiment

Our bung rolled on the floor and it took us ages to find it. Mr Simms told us to stop messing about and to get on with it.

Reported opinions

What we had to do was quite easy. The test tube had to have some water in it and then we put some detergent into the water using that thing. Then we had to shake it up. We forgot to put the bung in the first time so the water went all over and I got wet.

First person, past tense

Mr Simms wasn't very sympathetic! Anyway, the next time we remembered the bung and we made quite a bit of foam. I think that was when we used the river water but it might have been the tap water.

Unreliable reporting

I can't really remember. We had to do this with each type of water and I think the tap water made the most foam.

Get started

Discuss these questions and complete the tasks with a partner.

1. Explain in your own words the difference between a fact and an opinion.

2. Give an example of a fact. Give an example of an opinion.

3. How many suitable text types can you think of for reporting facts? Make a list.

4. Are some text types more fact-focused than others? Discuss.

5. Diary entries tend to focus on thoughts, feelings and opinions as well as recording events. Is the information in a diary entry always reliable? Are diaries unsuitable for recording facts?

Try these

The two accounts of the same experiment have been written very differently. Answer these questions about them.

1. What text features are present in Lynn's recount?

2. How has Lynn organised her writing?

3. What person and tense has Lynn written in?

4. What text features are present in Kate's science report?

5. What text feature does Kate use to emphasise the order of events?

6. Why does Kate use imperative verbs in the Method section of her report?

7. What imperative verbs does Kate use? Make a list.

8. How has Kate presented her results?

9. Which text is the most appropriate way to present scientific research?

10. Which text is most appropriate for a diary entry?

Now try these

1. Think of a science experiment you or your class has conducted. (If you can't think of any, think of one you would like to conduct.) Write a paragraph or two describing the experiment, similar to Lynn's recount. Describe what you did in the order that you did it, using the first person and past tense.

   Include answers to these questions about the experiment.

   a) What was the aim of the experiment?

   b) What equipment or resources were used?

   c) What did you do?

   d) What were the results?

   e) Did you prove or disprove anything?

2. Write a science report for your experiment. Set it out like Kate's science report: use the same sub-headings for each section; present the equipment in a bullet-point list; write the method as a numbered set of instructions; present the results in a table (if appropriate); write the aim and conclusion in full sentences.

Journalism

Journalism is writing and producing newspapers and magazines. People who write for newspapers and magazines are called **journalists**. Here is the front page of a newspaper.

Read the article, then answer the questions that follow.

LATEST NEWS

THE HERALD

ON THE MOON!

And It's "A Giant Leap for Mankind"

By John Barbour

21 July, 1969

SPACE CENTER – Houston – Two Americans landed and walked on the moon on Sunday, the first human beings on its alien soil.

They planted their nation's flag and talked to their President on Earth by radio-telephone.

MILLIONS ON THEIR HOME planet 240,000 miles away watched on television as they saluted the flag and scouted the lunar surface.

The first to step on the moon was Neil Armstrong, 38. He stepped onto the dusty surface at 9.56 p.m. His first words were, "That's one small step for a man, one giant leap for mankind".

Twenty minutes later, his companion, Edwin E. (Buzz) Aldrin Jr, 39, stepped to the surface. His words were, "Beautiful, beautiful. A magnificent desolation."

They had landed on the moon nearly seven hours before, at 3.18 p.m.

ARMSTRONG'S STEPS WERE cautious at first. He almost shuffled.

"The surface is fine and powdered, like powdered charcoal to the soles of the foot," he said. "I can see the footprints of my boots in the fine sandy particles."

Armstrong read from the plaque on the side of the Eagle, the spacecraft that had brought them to the surface. In a steady voice he said, "Here man first set foot on the moon, July 1969. We came in peace for all mankind."

AMERICANS FIRST TO WALK ON DEAD LUNAR SURFACE

ARMSTRONG APPEARED PHOSPHORESCENT in the blinding sunlight. He walked carefully at first in the gravity of the moon, only one-sixth as strong as on Earth. Then he tried wide gazelle-like leaps. In the lesser gravity of the moon, each of the men, 165 pounders on Earth, weighed something over 25 pounds on the moon. Armstrong began the rock picking on the lunar surface. Aldrin joined him using a small scoop to put lunar soil in a plastic bag.

Above them, invisible and nearly ignored, was Air Force Lt Col. Michael Collins, 38, keeping his lonely patrol around the moon till the moment his companions blast-off and return to him for the trip back home.

Get started

Discuss these questions and complete the tasks with a partner.

1. Explain in your own words what is meant by 'journalism'. Give examples to support your answer.

2. What do you think the job of a journalist might involve? Is journalism a job you would enjoy?

3. How important do you think journalism is? Explain your answer and give examples if you can.

4. Is it important for journalists to always tell the truth? Should they always present a balanced opinion?

5. Should journalists be allowed to publish anything they want to? Is there anything you think journalists shouldn't be allowed to publish? Who do you think has the right to decide?

Try these

When writing a news report, it is useful to plan by answering five questions. Practise this with reference to the newspaper report about the moon landings.

1. **What** is being reported?

2. **Where** is this happening?

3. **When** did it happen?

4. **Why** did it happen?

5. **Who** was involved?

Newspaper reports also contain direct speech, or quotes, from the people in the story.

6. List all the examples of direct speech in the moon landing report.

Now try these

1. Imagine you are a journalist for a local newspaper. Plan an article for the paper based on one of these events:

   • A storm has hit a seaside town.

   • The famous pop group 'All Directions' performed in town last night.

   • The local football team 'The Reds' has won a place in the FA Cup.

   Invent a headline to catch the readers' attention. Plan your report by using the five Ws: What? Where? When? Why? Who? Decide who you will interview. These people will provide quotes.

2. Using the ideas and notes from your planning, write the full newspaper report. Describe the event as it happened and include quotes from the people who were there.

Humorous stories

A humorous story is a story that depicts funny characters or incidents. They're often about things that are impossible and because they are impossible they are funny, rather than disturbing. This is the beginning of a story called **'Flat Stanley'**.

Read the extract from **'Flat Stanley' by Jeff Brown**, then answer the questions that follow.

> A silly surname invented for comic effect.

"I will go and wake the boys," Mrs Lambchop said to her husband, George Lambchop. Just then their younger son, Arthur, called from the bedroom he shared with his brother Stanley.

"Hey! Come and look! Hey!"

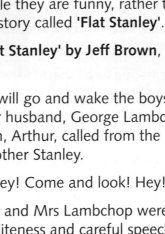

Mr and Mrs Lambchop were both very much in favour of politeness and careful speech. "Hay is for horses, Arthur, not people," Mr Lambchop said as they entered the bedroom. "Try to remember that."

"Excuse me," Arthur said. "But look!"

He pointed to Stanley's bed. Across it lay the enormous bulletin board that Mr Lambchop had given the boys a Christmas ago, so that they could pin up pictures and messages and maps. It had fallen during the night, on top of Stanley.

But Stanley was not hurt. In fact he would still have been sleeping if he had not been woken by his brother's shout.

"What's going on here?" he called out cheerfully from beneath the enormous board.

Mr and Mrs Lambchop hurried to lift it from the bed.

> Reactions to Stanley's accident are all weirdly calm. This is a technique called 'understatement'.

"Heavens!" said Mrs Lambchop.

"Gosh!" said Arthur. "Stanley's flat!"

"As a pancake," said Mr Lambchop. "Darndest thing I've ever seen."

"Let's all have breakfast," Mrs Lambchop said. "Then Stanley and I will go and see Doctor Dan and hear what he has to say."

The examination was almost over.

"How do you feel?" Doctor Dan asked. "Does it hurt very much?"

"I felt sort of tickly for a while after I got up," Stanley Lambchop said, "but I feel fine now."

"Well, that's mostly how it is with these cases," said Doctor Dan. "We'll just have to keep an eye on this young fellow," he said when he had finished the examination. "Sometimes we doctors, despite all our years of training and experience, can only marvel at how little we really know."

Mrs Lambchop said she thought that Stanley's clothes would have to be altered by the tailor now, so Doctor Dan told his nurse to take Stanley's measurements. Mrs Lambchop wrote them down.

Stanley was four feet tall, about a foot wide and half an inch thick.

When Stanley got used to being flat, he really enjoyed it.

He could go in and out of a room, even when the door was closed, just by lying down and sliding thorough the crack at the bottom.

Mr and Mrs Lambchop said it was silly, but they were quite proud of him.

Arthur got jealous and tried to slide under the door but he just banged his head.

Being flat could also be helpful, Stanley found.

He was taking a walk with Mrs Lambchop one afternoon when her favourite ring fell from her finger. The ring rolled across the pavement and down between the bars of a grating that covered a dark deep shaft. Mrs Lambchop began to cry.

"I have an idea," Stanley said. He took the laces out of his shoes and an extra pair out of his pocket and tied them all together to make one long lace. Then he tied the end of that to [...] his belt and gave the other end to his mother ...

Get started

Discuss these questions and complete the tasks with a partner.

1. What do you think makes a humorous or funny story?

2. Have you ever read any? What's the funniest thing you have ever heard, seen or read?

3. Discuss stories, cartoons, films and television programmes that you find funny.

4. Tell your partner a joke. Listen to their joke. Were your jokes funny? Why? / Why not?

Try these

Complete these tasks and answer the questions about the extract.

1. Describe in your own words what a humorous story is.

2. Give an example of understatement in this story.

3. Give an example of the use of contrast in this story.

4. If a boy were crushed in real life, how would you expect people to react?

5. How do the Lambchop family react to Stanley being flattened?

6. "Lambchop" is a silly surname. What do lamb chops make you think of?

7. What do you notice about the language the Lambchops use?

8. Which events in the story happen often in real life? Which events could never happen? Copy and complete the table with examples from the story.

Realistic everyday things	Things that could never happen

Now try these

1. Have you ever found yourself in a funny situation? Has a friend or member of your family ever told you about a funny situation or incident they were involved in? Why was it funny? Think about the situation and replay it in your mind so you are clear on the storyline. If nothing funny has ever happened to you or anyone you know, you will have to invent a humorous situation or think back to something you read or watched. Plan your story by thinking about the features of humorous stories you noted earlier.

    You should consider:

    * silly names or surnames

    * understatement

    * a contrast between the ordinary and the bizarre

    * impossible events

    * unusual behaviour.

2. Now write your humorous story. Use the notes you made previously and pay attention to the techniques you use to make it funny. Once you have finished, test your story on a partner. Give it to them to read or read it to them. Do they think it's funny? Were there any bits that didn't work? Make any improvements and then test it again on someone else.

Poems on similar themes

Poets may write about the same subject in a different way and you, as the reader, will respond differently to the same subject.

Read **'The Loner' by Julie Holder** and **'The New Boy' by John Walsh**, then answer the questions that follow.

The Loner

He leans against the playground wall,
Smacks his hands against the bricks
And other boredom-beating tricks,
Traces patterns with his feet,
Scuffs to make the tarmac squeak,
Back against the wall he stays –
And never plays.

The playground's quick with life.
The beat is strong.
Though sharp as a knife
Strife doesn't last long.
There is shouting, laughter, song,
And a place at the wall
For who won't belong.

We pass him running, skipping, walking,
In slow huddled groups, low-talking.
Each in our own familiar clique
We pass him by and never speak,
His loneliness is his shell and shield
And neither he or we will yield.

He wasn't there at the wall today,
Someone said he'd moved away
To another school and place
And on the wall where he used to lean
Someone had chalked
'watch this space'.

The New Boy

The door swung inward. I stood and breathed
The new-school atmosphere;
The smell and polish of disinfectant,
And the flavour of my own fear.

I followed into the cloakroom; the walls
Rang to the shattering noise
Of boys who barged and boys who banged;
Boys and still more boys!

A boot flew by. It's angry owner
Pursued with force and yell;
Somewhere a man snapped orders; somewhere
There clanged a warning bell.

And there I hung with my new schoolmates;
They pushing and shoving me; I
Unknown, unwanted, pinned to the wall;
On the verge of ready-to-cry.

Then from the doorway, a boy called out;
"Hey, You over there! You're new!
Don't just stand there propping the wall up!
I'll look after you!"

I turned; timidly raised my eyes;
He stood and grinned meanwhile;
And my fear dies, and my lips answered
Smile for his smile.

He showed me the basins, the rows of pegs;
He hung my cap at the end;
He led me away to my new classroom ...
And now that boy's my friend.

Get started

Discuss these questions and complete the tasks with a partner.

1. What is the main theme of both these poems? Find examples to support your answer.

2. Do you have a favourite poem? How many more poems do you know? What are they about?

3. Copy and complete the table. Make a list of all the poems you can think of and what each poem is about.

Poem	What the poem is about

4. Do any of the poems you've listed cover the same topics, themes or issues? If so, do they deal with them in the same way or differently? Compare and contrast any poems that deal with the same topics, themes or issues.

Try these

Complete these tasks and answer the questions about the poems.

1. Copy and complete the table to compare the structures of the two poems.

	The Loner	The New Boy
Number of verses		
Number of lines per verse		
Rhyme scheme		

2. In 'The Loner,' what is meant by describing the boy's loneliness as his "shell" and his "shield"?

3. Make a list of the verbs in verses 2, 3 and 4 of 'The New Boy'.

4. What effect do these verbs have?

5. How does each poem describe the atmosphere at school? Are the descriptions similar?

6. Compare the endings of the poems. Are they happy, sad or something else?

7. How well do you feel you get to know the lonely boy in 'The Loner'?

8. Which poem do you like best? Why?

Now try these

1. Plan your own poem on the theme of loneliness. It does not have to be set in a school. Make notes on these things as you plan your poem.

   • Theme: loneliness

   • Setting:

   • Character(s):

   • Verses:

   • Rhyme scheme:

   • Powerful vocabulary:

   • Figurative language: (similes, metaphors, personification, alliteration)

   • Point of view:

2. Using your notes, write your poem on the theme of loneliness. When it is written, 'perform' your poem by recording it or reading it to a partner. Take feedback from your partner and do the same for them and their poem. If you have recorded your poem, listen back to it. What have you done well? Could you improve anything?

Extended stories

The longer a story is, the harder it is to keep track of its various elements. Long stories are usually broken up into chapters. Long stories need a good structure in each chapter as well as a good structure overall. This is why it is so important to plan a story. Here's a story plan for the first two chapters of a book called **'An Unusual Find'**.

Read these story plans for two chapters of a book, then answer the questions that follow.

Chapter 1

Setting	Characters	Plot
On a farm – kitchen scene where characters are having their breakfast: cheerful / bright / clean, old-fashioned dresser with dinner service, flowers on table	3 children: Sam aged 8 – rather timid, scares easily, not sure of himself. Small, red hair, freckles, dressed in shorts and football top Jo aged 10 – Sam's sister, tomboy, very confident, adventurous. Red hair very short, tall for age, dressed in jeans and T-shirt Martin aged 12 – serious-looking boy, elder brother of Jo and Sam. Wears spectacles, dark hair, dressed in jeans and checked shirt	Introduction – describe the scene and the children Conversation over breakfast – what are they going to do today? Reader must learn that they are on holiday at auntie's house. Bring out the children's different characters through what they say and how they act – Jo wants to climb trees. Sam and Martin are not keen.

Chapter 2

Setting	Characters	Plot
Same setting – kitchen	As Chapter 1 Introduce new character: Auntie Betty – middle-aged, cheerful, hard-working, always busy. Wears a dress and an apron. Hair long but tied up in a bun Anxious for the children to finish breakfast so she can clear away and get on with her work	Auntie Betty comes into the kitchen as the children are talking about what they're going to do. She suggests exploring and finding their way around the farm. Children agree
Move outside, describe farmyard		They go outside but can find nothing interesting until Jo spots the barn
Move to barn – cold and gloomy with rusting machinery, hay, somewhat run down		Jo eager to go in, Sam unwilling. Martin agrees but seems uninterested. Look around inside
Old cupboard, paint peeling off, looks discarded but is locked		Jo spots an old cupboard in the corner. Finds it locked and decides to break in. Martin warns her not to but she takes no notice Jo opens cupboard with a piece of metal – strange light and sounds come from opened cupboard

Get started

Discuss these questions and complete the tasks with a partner.

1. What books have you read with chapters? Think of examples of chapter books you have read.

2. Why do you think longer stories are divided into chapters?

3. Think of a book with chapters that you have read and describe the first two chapters to a partner. Listen to your partner do the same.

4. Discuss the chapters you described. What do the first two chapters of both books have in common? What characters and plot elements are introduced?

Try these

Complete these tasks and answer the questions about the story plans.

1. What would you expect to find in the planning of the first two chapters of an extended story? Make a list by selecting the correct statements.

   - characters' personalities
   - direct speech
   - how the final chapter will end
   - descriptions of settings
   - character descriptions
   - structure of the whole story
   - details of the plot up to the end of the second chapter

2. Which three story elements have been included in the example plans?

3. What other elements might you want to include in a story plan?

4. Where is Chapter 1 set? Where does the setting move to in Chapter 2?

5. What character details are included in the Characters planning sections?

6. What must the reader learn in Chapter 1?

7. Who is the new character introduced in Chapter 2?

8. How has the author planned to end Chapter 2?

Now try these

1. Reread the story plans so far. At the end of Chapter 2, the author has planned for the children to find strange lights and sounds coming from an opened cupboard. What do the children find in the cupboard? Plan Chapter 3 under these headings:

   • What is in the cupboard: (make it something exciting)

   • What they do next / where they go: (invent a new setting)

   • Introduce a new character: (create a villain)

   • Chapter ending: (make it a cliff-hanger)

   Write the chapter in full using your plan, to continue from the end of Chapter 2.

2. Plan and write Chapter 4, the final chapter. Plan the ending, deciding what type of narrative ending you want to use. Read it through, checking for effect. Is there anything you would like to improve?

Explanations

To explain something is to make something clear by providing the relevant facts. Diaries and instructions can both be explanation texts. Diaries have the advantage of being a very flexible form of writing, with any details the writer wants to include. They can explain how or why things have happened (in the past). Instructions are a rigid form of writing with a specific purpose. They explain to the reader how to do something, step by step, in the present. Here are two explanations for pitching a tent.

Read the diary and the information text, then answer the questions that follow.

This is a page from a diary written by Tom, describing how he and his friend Sundeep pitched their tent.

Describe an event

Reported speech

Record memories, thoughts and feelings

Personal pronouns

Full sentences and paragraphs

When we were given our tent, we emptied everything from the bag onto the ground. There were a lot of different bits, so we sorted everything out into piles. We said to each other that it was a good thing it wasn't raining, or all the equipment would have got wet and muddy.

First we sorted out the sections for the tent poles. There were three poles and each one had three sections. When we had fixed them together, I climbed inside the inner tent and put the pointed end through the hole in the ridge of the tent. By now the wind was beginning to blow and Sundeep was having difficulty hanging on to the guy ropes outside.

Next we fixed the ridge pole between the two upright poles, which was a bit fiddly. We soon realised it was better for one of us to hold the pole while the other banged in the pegs and tied the guy ropes. The last thing we needed to do was put the outer tent over the ridge pole, and before we knew it we could crawl inside and were all warm and snug out of the wind, that is, until we realised we hadn't put in all the pegs along the side. By now it was raining and we got very wet!

Here are the instructions for assembling the tent, written for others to read and follow.

When pitching a tent, all the tent components should be placed on a dry area of ground, or onto a plastic sheet if available. The various items should be sorted so each is easily to hand when required.

The inner tent should be positioned so that a pre-assembled upright tent pole can be threaded into the ridge at the top of the tent. Similarly, position the other pole before a second person outside the tent places the pre-assembled ridge pole between the two uprights and holds the whole structure in position. The first person fixes the guy ropes to pegs positioned either side of both the front and rear of the tent, as indicated in the diagram.

Finally, the rest of the tent is firmly fixed with pegs to secure it against strong winds.

Get started

Discuss these questions and complete the tasks with a partner.

1. In your own words, define what an explanation is.

2. What different formats could you use to explain something? Make a list.

3. What are the advantages and disadvantages to each format?

4. What is the best format for explaining how to do something?

5. What are the best text formats for explaining your personal motives for doing something?

Try these

Complete these tasks and answer the questions about the two texts.

1. Who is the intended reader of Tom's diary entry?

2. Who is the intended reader of the instructions?

3. Which text records memories, thoughts and feelings?

4. What is the aim of an instruction text?

5. How is Tom's diary entry structured?

6. What is missing from the instruction text that should be there?

7. Why is the order of things important in an instruction text?

8. Why does the instructions text use the word "should" a lot?

9. What text features in Tom's diary entry do not appear in the instructions? Make a list.

10. What features does the instruction text contain? Write a list.

Now try these

1. Tom writes a recount (his diary entry) about making a camp fire. Once it is made, he will cook his tea. Think of a time when you made a meal or some item of food. What ingredients and equipment did you need? What step-by-step instructions did you use in order to make your food? Write the set of instructions so that someone else might be able to follow them.

2. Write your diary entry about the time you made this item of food. Remember that a diary account will:

   • describe the event;

   • record your thoughts and feelings at the time;

   • be written in the past tense;

   • contain connecting words and phrases.

Paragraphs in non-fiction

Longer pieces of text should be divided into **paragraphs**. A paragraph is a section of text indicated by a new line. It usually comprises more than one sentence and deals with a single theme, topic or idea. Each paragraph usually has two or more sentences related to the same idea.

Read these information texts, then answer the questions that follow.

Usain Bolt

Paragraphs organise information and break up the text into readable chunks.

Jamaican sprinter Usain Bolt is arguably the fastest man in the world, winning three gold medals at the 2008 Olympic Games in Beijing, China, and becoming the first man in Olympic history to win both the 100 m and 200 m races in record times. He continued his run of success by winning three gold medals at the London 2012 Olympics, defending both of his sprint titles – 100 and 200 metres – and, with his team mates, retaining the 4×100 m relay title in a world record time of 36.84 seconds.

Usain's early life

Bolt's successes are listed chronologically.

He was born in Jamaica on 21 August, 1986. From a young age, he was a very good cricketer as well as a remarkable young sprinter. By the age of 14, Bolt had won his first school championships medal, taking the silver in the 200 m race.

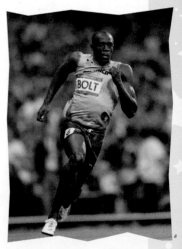

At the age of 15, Bolt won his first international competition at the 2002 World Junior Championships. He won the 200 m race, making him the youngest world-junior gold medal winner ever! People realised he was a very special athlete and he soon was given the nickname Lightning Bolt!

His running career

Despite being constantly troubled by injury, he was chosen for the Jamaican Olympic squad for the 2004 Olympics but was eliminated in the first round due to that recurring injury.

In 2005, he made the difficult decision to move to a new coach, Glenn Mills. This was a good move but, unfortunately, injuries continued to be a problem.

But by 2007 things were improving. First, he broke the 30-year-old Jamaican 200 m record and then won two silver medals at the World Championships in Japan.

Bolt strikes gold

At the Beijing Olympics in 2008, Usain broke the 100 m world record, winning in 9.69 seconds. Not only did he run a very fast time, but everyone was amazed that he slowed down to celebrate before he finished! He also won gold medals in the 200 m race and in the relay.

At the 2012 Olympic Games in London, he won his fourth Olympic gold medal in the men's 100 m race, beating his friend and rival Yohan Blake. This was not a new Olympic record. The win marked Bolt's second consecutive gold medal in the 100 m.

He went on to compete in the men's 200 m, claiming his second consecutive gold medal in that race too. He was awarded his third gold medal as part of the Jamaican relay team.

Bolt expressed his pride about his 2012 performance, saying, "It's what I came here to do. I've got nothing left to prove."

New section of text, indicated by the heading

Space between paragraphs

Mo Farah

Although Mohamed Farah was born in Mogadishu on 23 March 1983, his father had been born in England and had met his mother when on holiday in Somalia. Mo moved to London when he was eight years old. His first love was football, but it was his speed on the pitch that showed a special talent for running. (More than anything Mo dreamed of playing for Arsenal!) When he was 13, Mo came ninth in the English schools cross country competition, but by the following year he won – and went on to win four more English school titles. In 2005, Mo Farah made the important decision to move in with a group of Kenyan runners that included 10,000 m world number one Micah Kogo. "I don't just want to be British number one, I want to be up there with the best," said Mo. Soon after, he became Britain's second-fastest 5000 m runner and came second in the European Championships before winning the European Cross-Country Championship in Italy. The 2008 Olympics weren't good for Mo, but he really started to improve dramatically after going to Ethiopia and Kenya for training. He set a new British indoor record in the 3000 m. Soon after, he broke his own record by more than six

seconds, which commentator Steve Cram called "the best performance by a male British distance runner for a generation". However, he became unwell after several races and it was eventually found that he had low levels of important chemicals in his blood. Once this was sorted out, he started to win more important races. He won the 2010 London 10,000 m in a British record and the following week he won the European Cup 10,000 m and then the 2010 European Athletics Championships, where he took the 10,000 m gold medal. 2011 proved to be a highly successful year. In January he won the Edinburgh Cross Country. Then in February 2011, he moved to the USA, to work with his new coach. He went on to win major races all over the world. Dave Moorcroft, former 5000 m world-record holder, described Farah as "the greatest distance runner that Britain has ever seen". On 4 August 2012, he won the 10,000 m gold, Great Britain's first ever Olympic gold medal in the 10,000 m. A week later Farah made it a long-distance double, winning the 5000 m. This was when millions of people all over the world saw Mo's unique victory celebration dance – the Mobot!

Get started

Discuss these questions and complete the tasks with a partner.

1. Explain in your own words what is meant by the term 'paragraph'.

2. Why is it important to use paragraphs in non-fiction writing?

3. Look back at your previous writing and find examples of when you used paragraphs and explain why you used them.

4. Discuss whether your reasons are the same for fiction and non-fiction.

5. Make a checklist for the use of paragraphs in non-fiction. Use the annotations on the extracts for help if you need to.

Try these

Complete these tasks and answer the questions about the texts.

1. How many headings are there in the text about Usain Bolt?

2. How many paragraphs are there in the text about Usain Bolt?

3. Write a sentence to summarise each section of the text about Usain Bolt.

4. Look at the text on Mohamed Farah. What is wrong with it?

5. How would you break up the information in the text on Mohamed Farah? Copy the table and add these headings to it in the correct order. One has been done for you. Then specify where you think each paragraph break should go.

> British records and European champion
> 2012: Double Olympic champion
> His ambition grows
> Mo's early life
> Britain's greatest male distance runner

Heading	Information to be included in this section
Mo's early life	Up to "... English school titles"

Now try these

1. Plan an information text about your favourite hobby or sport. The facts for your information text need to be organised into sections. Here is a diagram with ideas for the different sections of your information text. Copy the diagram and fill in any or all of the sections with information about your chosen hobby or sport. Add other sections with ideas of your own if you want to. Research your hobby or sport if you need to and check that the information is accurate and correct.

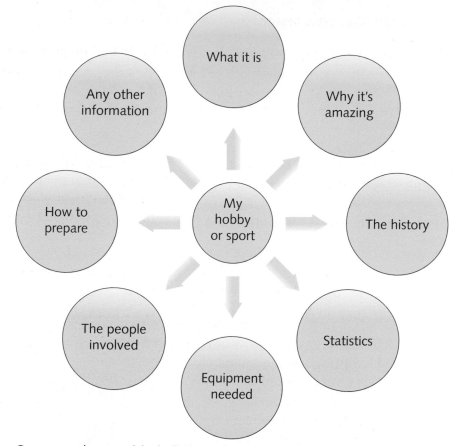

Once you have added all the information you want to include in your text, decide the order in which you want to write the information. Label each section with a number according to the order in which you're going to write the information.

2. Using your plan, write an information text about your chosen hobby or sport. Use the checklist you composed to make sure you are using sections and paragraphs correctly.

Paragraphs in fiction

Paragraphs are used in fiction writing whenever the narrative changes time, place, topic or speaker, or when the writer wants to control the pace of the narrative and create dramatic effects.

Read the story extract, then answer the questions that follow.

Our New Home

Mum closed the car door. Everything had been packed into the car, including us, and it was time to go. I felt a rush of emotions as the car pulled out of the drive. We were leaving our home. I was 15 years old and had lived in that house all of my life.

Change in topic (also change in time)

When dad disappeared, mum said we couldn't afford to live there anymore. I had tried to argue with her, talk her out of moving away, but she told me there was no point. These were the facts, she'd said, and we all had to face them.

A very short paragraph for dramatic effect; it is a moment of heightened emotion

I watched as the house seemed to disappear behind a mist of fog. In fact, it wasn't fog; they were my tears.

The day seemed to roll by as we travelled along the motorway. My younger brother Kirk, he was only five, kept on tapping his hand against the window. He was playing some sort of game and to be honest the sound was really annoying. Mum didn't say anything though. She hadn't spoken since we left the house.

She hadn't spoken much at all these last few months. It was like the breath had been knocked out of her. Looking at her sideways, from the passenger seat next to her, I tried to work out how much she'd really changed. Was she as different as I thought? Or did I just see her differently now?

Character begins to speak

"Mum ..." I began. But she just drove, quietly humming to herself. It wasn't a real tune; it was just a sound. More like a stifled groan. I put my headphones on and turned up my music.

Different time

It was getting dark. We would soon be there, at "our new home," as Mum kept on calling it. I didn't want a new home. I wanted the old one with all of my friends and with Mr Andrews's grumpy dog jumping over the back fence. In fact, Mr Andrews was grumpier than his dog. The only difference was that he hadn't learned to bark yet. I smiled to myself. It's funny the things you miss.

Different place

We pulled into the drive. At last Kirk was quiet. Perhaps he was secretly nervous too, behind all of that dribble and noise, about beginning a new life. I looked up at the new house through the car window. What would our new lives be like?

Get started

Discuss these questions and complete the tasks with a partner.

1. Look back at your previous writing and find examples of when you used paragraphs in fiction writing. Explain why you used them.

2. Make a checklist for the use of paragraphs in fiction writing. Read the notes and annotations of the extract for further support, if you need to.

3. Look at examples of fiction texts (in books you are reading or that are available to you). What is the shortest paragraph you can find? What is the longest paragraph you can find? What effect do short paragraphs have? What effect do long paragraphs have? Can you identify the reasons for paragraph breaks in the texts you are looking at? Are there any you don't understand? Are there any you disagree with?

Try these

1. Copy and complete the table. For each paragraph of the story, write the first sentence and the reason for starting a new paragraph.

	First sentence	Reason for starting a new paragraph
Paragraph 2		
Paragraph 3		
Paragraph 4		
Paragraph 5		
Paragraph 6		
Paragraph 7		
Paragraph 8		

2. What happens next? Write the next three paragraphs of the story. Use your checklist to help you remember when to start a new paragraph. Make a note of your reason for each paragraph break.

Now try these

1. In this narrative extract, the paragraph breaks have been omitted. Using the line numbers, suggest where you think the paragraph breaks should happen and give your reasons.

1	It was a cold, damp day. The rain had been falling all morning and
2	there had been no chance of going out at all. Kamal really wanted
3	to meet his friends and play football. But here he was, stuck inside
4	with no sign of brighter weather. He would have to stay indoors and
5	watch the television. All of a sudden the phone rang in the other
6	room and he ran to answer it. It was his cousin, Hamid, asking him to
7	come over to play on his new computer game. It had been a present
8	for his birthday and he was longing for someone to play it with him.
9	The offer was irresistible! Kamal agreed, promising to be there in
10	half an hour. He rushed to the hall to get his coat and search for his
11	trainers. It was then he remembered the hole! The last time he wore
12	his trainers playing football he had noticed large holes in the soles of
13	both trainers, made worse by continually playing football! His feet
14	would get soaked but that new game was something special and
15	he couldn't resist the invitation. He put them on, opened the door
16	and rushed outside. Rain fell in sheets, and a cold wind blew, but
17	still Kamal ran on to his cousin's house. By the time he reached the
18	end of his road, his feet were soaked through. His socks were wet,
19	his toes were freezing cold and he felt sure there was a blister on his
20	left heel. He saw his cousin's house in the distance and leaping over
21	puddles like small lakes he finally rang the door bell. "Hello Kamal,"
22	said his cousin. "You'd better come in and get dry. I don't know what
23	we can do though; there's been a power cut due to the storm and
24	the computer isn't working." The look on Kamal's face said it all.
25	Cold, wet and no computer game. What a day!

2. Write your own short story. Your paragraphs must structure the story. Use your checklist to help you. Choose one of these titles or use one of your own:

   • The lost purse

   • The match

   • Aliens in the High Street!

Writing for different purposes

When you have researched a topic, there are different ways to convey factual information including diaries, letters, reports, newspaper articles, maps and diagrams. The method chosen depends on who will be reading it and what they need to know. Here are three different ways of giving information about Morocco.

Read the information on Morocco, then answer the questions that follow.

From an information book

Use of semicolons

Full sentences

Sub-headings

Morocco

Location

The name Morocco comes from the old Arabic phrase "Maghreb al-Aksa" meaning "The Land of the Furthest West"; Morocco

is, in fact, at the extreme western corner of North Africa. It is the only North African country with a coast facing the Atlantic Ocean, and of all the North African countries, it is the nearest to Europe. The country is bordered inland by Algeria, and for a much shorter distance by Western Sahara.

Size

The area of Morocco is 440,000 square kilometres (170,000 square miles). This is just a little more than twice as large as the area of the British Isles.

The mountains

Well over one-third of Morocco is mountainous. In the north are the Rif Mountains; further south are the Middle Atlas, the High Atlas and the Anti Atlas. All these ranges, except the

Rif, run roughly southwest to northeast across the country. In the east, the Middle Atlas and High Atlas merge to form a barren tableland.

From an atlas

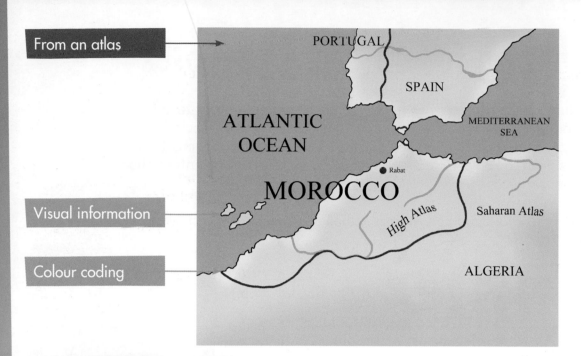

PORTUGAL

SPAIN

ATLANTIC OCEAN

MEDITERRANEAN SEA

● Rabat

MOROCCO

High Atlas

Saharan Atlas

ALGERIA

Visual information

Colour coding

From a reference book

A list of statistics

Morocco

Population: about 20 million

Main languages: Arabic and French

Main religion: Islam

Capital: Rabat

Area: 440,000 square kilometres (170,000 square miles)

Highest mountain: Tidiguin: 2,400 metres

Chief produce: fruit (oranges and figs), cereals

Information is organised using a colon.

Get started

Discuss these questions and complete the tasks with a partner.

1. Think of as many different ways to present information as you can. Make a list.

2. How do you know which method to use when presenting information? What are the advantages and disadvantages of the different ways you have thought of?

3. When and how can you use a colon? Write the rules. (If you're not sure about them, look them up.)

4. When and how can you use a semicolon? Write the rules. (If you're not sure about them, look them up.)

Try these

Answer these questions.

1. What are the advantages of using a map to present information?

2. What are the disadvantages of using a map to present information?

3. What do the pictures in the information book show the reader?

4. What facts are included in the information book extract? Make a list.

5. What three pieces of information can only be found in the map?

6. What piece of information is in both the information book and the reference book?

7. What could be added to the map to give the reader an idea of the size of Morocco?

8. Which extract uses colons to organise information?

9. What are the sub-headings for in the information book?

Now try these

1. Imagine you work for the Moroccan tourist board and you have to write an information leaflet promoting Morocco as a place to visit. Read through the information in the extracts provided and, if possible, do your own research and make notes about places to visit and things to do while in Morocco. Your leaflet should encourage visitors to come and see Morocco. What facts and information will you include to make people want to visit? Decide what the sections will be and how you will present the information leaflet. Consider layout, maps, illustrations, bullet point lists and anything else you can think of.

2. Write the leaflet, referring to the notes you made earlier. Remember, you want people to visit Morocco so use persuasive language and tell them enticing things. Use organisational features to format the information you're providing. Think carefully about how you present the different types of information. Try to make your leaflet as reader-friendly and usable as possible.

Story endings

How you, as a reader, feel when you finish a story depends on how the story ends. Writers know how they want to make their readers feel and they write the endings to their stories to produce these feelings. Here is a plan for a story called **'The Mountain Climbers'**.

Read the story plan, then answer the questions that follow.

Beginning

Three climbers are half way up a mountain when one falls. He is saved from plummeting to the bottom by a ledge, but his leg is broken.

Middle

The three climbers spend an uncomfortable night on the mountain. The temperature drops and the man with the broken leg becomes very ill. Rescue is a remote possibility because, foolishly, they didn't tell anyone they were going climbing.

A happy ending where everything works out	**Ending**
	Do you want to leave your reader with a sense of relief?
	One climber has a flare so the climbers are rescued.
A cliff-hanger ending (a dramatic ending to a story that maintains suspense)	**Do you want to leave your reader in suspense?**
	Two of the climbers go down the mountain to get help, leaving the injured man alone. Will they return?
	Do you want to leave your reader with a sense of "if only"?
A sad ending	A rescue party does arrive but too late to save the injured man.

Get started

Discuss these questions and complete the tasks with a partner.

1. Describe some endings of stories you have read, watched or listened to.

2. Which endings did you like best? Do you prefer happy endings or sad endings? Do you enjoy a good cliff hanger? Have you enjoyed any mysterious endings that have left you with questions unanswered?

3. Write a few sentences explaining how you like stories to end. Is a happy ending always the best ending?

Try these

What do you know about story endings?

1. Write a definition of the term 'cliff hanger'.

2. What is a 'prequel'? What is a 'sequel'?

3. Some stories are called 'cyclical'. What do you think this means for the ending of the story?

4. What is an 'ambiguous' ending?

5. What sorts of endings are most suitable for young children?

6. Copy and complete the table, describing how you might expect a story in each of these genres to end.

	How the story might end
A fairytale	
A murder mystery	
A romance	
A moral story	
A tragedy	
A comedy	
A survival story	

Now try these

1. Reread the three possible endings to 'The Mountain Climbers'. Think of another way the story could end. What effect will it have on the reader? Write a short description of what happens.

   Choose what you think is the best ending, one of the three suggestions or your own, and complete the story 'The Mountain Climbers' in full. Read it through, making sure that it creates the effect you wanted. Share the ending with a partner and listen to their feedback. Do the same for your partner's story ending.

2. Think of a story you have read, watched or listened to where you really didn't like the ending. Write a review of the story, explaining exactly why you didn't like the ending. Here are some questions to help you decide why you didn't like it:

   • Did the ending make sense?

   • Do you think it was planned well enough?

   • Did it seem false or not to fit with the rest of the story somehow?

   • Was it too sudden or abrupt, or just not really an ending at all?

   • Was it too complicated? Did too much happen at once?

   • Was the problem that questions were left unanswered and loose ends not tied up? If so, do you think that was deliberate or a mistake made by the author?

   • Is it just a matter of personal taste?